IN THE NAME OF THE LAW

(2nd Edition)

Rev. Dr. Gloria Lynn Sydnor Smith

ISBN: 978-1-959802-54-9

Dedication

[This book is dedicated to those who were denied a fair trial, wrongfully convicted, or endured injustice within the criminal legal system—and to the families and friends who carry that burden alongside them.]

Acknowledgment

To my beloved parents, The Rev. Dr. Calvin H. Sydnor III and The Rev. Dr. Charlotte A. Blake Sydnor, thank you for everything. I could not have asked for better role models. You raised us in faith, instilling values that shaped my journey. Though attending church was once an obligation, I now recognize it as one of the greatest gifts you gave me. The lessons, the foundation, and the unwavering support you provided continue to guide me, and for that, I am forever grateful.

To my spiritual father, Bishop Frederick A. Wright, Sr., and his loving wife, Episcopal Supervisor Jennifer Wright, thank you for standing with me at every pivotal moment in my ministry journey. From my license to preach to ordination as deacon and elder, through my doctoral defense and beyond, your unwavering support has been a priceless gift. I am forever grateful.

I thank God for igniting this fire within me, a passion that has fueled my work as both criminal defense attorney and pastor. By the grace of God, I earned a Doctorate in Ministry while serving in these dual callings. My dissertation, "Prophetic Preaching That Prepares a Congregation to Minister to Individuals That Have Been Incarcerated," laid the foundation for this book and deepened the burden that birthed it. Every step has been ordered by God. Every role has been sacred. To God be the glory.

CONTENT

Foreword

America claims to be the land of liberty, yet its foundation is built on bondage. The love of money, declared in Scripture as the root of all kinds of evil, has corrupted the nation's highest ideals. Though the 13th Amendment supposedly abolished chattel slavery, its exception clause left the door wide open: slavery wasn't abolished, it was repackaged. Today, those once called "slaves" are branded "criminals," "thugs," and "inmates."

The Dred Scott decision made it clear: Black people were not people, they were property. That ruling echoed through generations, shaping systems that criminalized Black existence from birth to death.

Black communities were the initial targets of mass incarceration, though today the system claims to be colorblind, blind only to equity, never to profit. The targets have expanded, like flames of a fire.

America's criminal justice system has become a billion-dollar enterprise that feeds on flesh. It's never been about justice, it's always about commerce. Bodies are counted and numbered, but their lives never matter. Stocks numbers rise while spirits are crushed. This "criminal justice" machine thrives not on righteousness, but on greed that doesn't see race, just opportunities to make more money.

In The Name of the Law is a challenge to this machinery. It examines how laws are the tools of the powerful to maintain power and to marginalize as many people as possible in the name of the law. This book does not whisper. It roars.

Introduction

"[3] And the scribes and Pharisees brought unto him a woman taken in adultery; and when they had set her in the midst, [4] They say unto him, Master, this woman was taken in adultery, in the very act. [5] Now Moses in the law commanded us, that such should be stoned: but what sayest thou?"

- John 8:3-5 (Ethiopian Bible)

Powerful people have been using the law to destroy other people for an exceptionally long time. If this practice continues, we are all at risk of devastation at the whim of a more powerful person.

Laws are meant to set boundaries that allow everyone to live in a safe environment.

About the Author

The Rev. Dr. Gloria Sydnor Smith is a criminal defense attorney and an ordained elder in the African Methodist Episcopal Church. She is married with four adult children. She enjoys singing, weightlifting, watching college football and basketball.

Chapter One – The Loophole

The 13th Amendment was ratified by the Senate on December 6, 1865. It did not abolish slavery. It says, in relevant part: Neither slavery nor involuntary servitude, *except* as a punishment for crime whereof the party shall have been duly convicted, shall exist within the United States, or any place subject to their jurisdiction.[1]

The loophole that failed to fully abolish slavery lies in the exception permitting forced labor as punishment for a crime upon conviction. This legal provision has long served as a tool for systemic oppression, allowing the law to perpetuate a new form of bondage. It has disproportionately ensnared Black Americans in the cycle of mass incarceration, where imprisonment functions as modern-day slavery. The system profits from the unpaid or underpaid labor of inmates while exploiting probationers through mandated excessive community service hours.

On the surface, probation sounds like a better option than prison. But for many, it's a delayed sentence disguised as grace. Some would rather serve six months behind bars than risk failing at five years of probation. They know the terms are stacked: maintain employment, pay fines and court costs, report regularly, sometimes weekly, to a probation officer, and submit to random drug screenings that require additional visits. And that's not all. Community service hours must be completed, and every condition met without a single misstep. In a

[1] U.S. Const. amend. XIII, § 1.

system built for surveillance, one missed appointment, one late payment, one failed test, and freedom folds back into incarceration.

This is a mechanism that fuels itself, growing larger and more entrenched year after year. While incarceration rates rise and probation rolls swell, the county builds new courthouses and rolls out fleets of gleaming vehicles. Justice is dressed in marble and chrome, while oppression operates in plain sight. The system expands not through reform, but through reinvestment.

Slavery built this nation from the dirt up, on the backs of stolen bodies and commodified labor. And today, that same system sustains the machinery, from county to county, state to state, all across this country. Slavery still exists; it hides in plain sight within the 13th Amendment's exception clause. The courtroom has become the new auction block, where Black bodies are processed, priced, and passed into bondage through plea deals and probation. The chains are cleaner now, but they're just as tight.

This system survives by starving what makes us human. It works when citizens are deprived of food, healthcare, housing, education, when survival becomes conditional, and dignity becomes negotiable. The less people have, the more control the system gains.

It works when the people are hungry. It works when healthcare is denied. It works when our children sit in classrooms with broken windows and outdated books. Because when basic human needs go unmet, bondage doesn't need chains, it just needs desperation. This is how the system multiplies: not just through incarceration, but through deprivation.

This system has been feeding itself for generations, growing stronger and more insatiable with each passing law, each plea deal, each prison contract. It's no longer just a system, it's a monster, engineered to ensnare almost anyone. But its appetite is racialized. It survives off Black bodies. It devours our labor, our presence, our pain. And that's why Black Americans have been cast as the perpetual boogie man, the fabricated threat used to justify the beast's existence. Not because of what we've done, but because of what the system demands: a villain to chase, a soul to cage, a body to brand.

These actions are cloaked in the legitimacy of state and federal law, but their foundation is rotten. They don't just uphold injustice; they reinforce it, leveraging the insidious loophole woven into the 13th Amendment. That exception, permitting slavery as punishment for a crime, has metastasized into a system that exploits, surveils, and subjugates. It allows oppression to masquerade as order, and bondage to masquerade as justice.

Slavery was not merely a historical atrocity, it was a malevolent force, echoing the ancient bondage of the Israelites in Egypt. Just as Pharaoh's heart hardened, defying justice until the land was struck with ten devastating plagues, oppression in this country has persisted, adapting and reshaping itself through generations. Freedom only came to the Israelites after the ultimate tragedy, the death of Pharaoh's firstborn son, alongside every firstborn in Egypt who was not shielded by the blood of the lamb. Likewise, true liberation in America remains elusive, as the spirit of slavery lingers, disguised within the machinery of law and power.

Nations and corporations were forged upon the brutal framework of slavery, reaping immense profits and accumulating generational wealth at the expense of human suffering. Laws were crafted, enacted, and upheld, not to dismantle oppression, but to fortify and legitimize it. Slavery was not merely allowed to exist; it was cultivated, expanded, and embedded into the very fabric of economies, flourishing for centuries under the guise of legality and progress.

In the landmark case of *Dred Scott v. Sandford*, 60 U.S. 393, decided on March 6, 1857, the United States Supreme Court delivered a devastating 7-2 ruling, authored by Chief Justice Roger B. Taney. The Court declared that Black people, whether enslaved or free, were not citizens and had no rights under the Constitution, instead viewing them solely as property. This decision not only denied Dred Scott his plea for freedom but also reinforced the legal framework of slavery, deepening racial injustice and fueling tensions that would ultimately lead to the Civil War.[2]

The *Dred Scott* decision declared that Black people were property, not persons with constitutional rights. And while its consequences were nullified by the 13th, 14th, and 15th Amendments, the Supreme Court itself never explicitly overturned the ruling. That silence matters. It means that if these Amendments were ever repealed or weakened, the logic of *Dred Scott* could crawl back into jurisprudence. A nightmare preserved in legal amber, waiting for erosion to make it law again.

---

[2] Dred Scott v. Sandford, 60 U.S. 393 (1857)

The fact remains: Black people were once declared property by the highest court in the land, a ruling never explicitly reversed. Instead of renouncing that sin, the system engraved a loophole into the 13th Amendment, allowing slavery to persist as punishment for crime. And now, the legacy continues. That loophole became a pipeline. The label shifted from 'property' to 'criminal,' but the result is the same, Black bodies funneled into cages, stripped of dignity, and offered up to a system that profits from their confinement.

The *Dred Scott* ruling still lingers like a ghost, unseen, unheard, but ever-present in the shadows of subsequent legal frameworks, shaping the undercurrents of systemic injustice. Chief Justice Taney said that the "negro race ... was doomed to slavery."[3] First, I rebuke that curse in the name of Jesus. Second, this legal curse was built upon the grotesque lie that Black people were not human, an ideology designed to justify perpetual subjugation.

The ruling did not simply deny freedom, it cemented dehumanization as a legal principle. When the law reduces a human being to property, it paves the way for atrocities like lynchings, and whole communities burned down to the ground, to be justified and upheld without consequences.

The dehumanization of Black people persists, transforming routine traffic stops into fatal encounters, where a moment of compliance or defiance can mean the difference between life and death. The routine acceptance of these unacceptable events is profoundly tragic.

---

[3] Dred Scott v, 60 U.S. at 407

The cruel logic of Dred Scott has been woven into the very fabric of this nation's legal and social structures, so deeply embedded that racial injustice not only thrives but is often ignored, dismissed, or denied, allowing oppression to persist under the guise of normalcy.

There is no clearer lens through which to grasp how deeply dehumanization seeped into the hearts and minds of this nation than Taney's words in Dred Scott:

"They had for more than a century before been regarded as beings of an inferior order, and altogether unfit to associate with the white race, either in social or political relations; and so far inferior, that they had no rights which the white man was bound to respect; and that the negro might justly and lawfully be reduced to slavery ... He was bought and sold, and treated as an ordinary article of merchandise and traffic, whenever a profit could be made by it. This opinion was at that time fixed and universal in the civilized portion of the white race. It was regarded as an axiom in morals as well as in politics, which no one thought of disputing, or supposed to be open to dispute; and men in every grade and position in society daily and habitually acted upon it in their private pursuits, as well as in matters of public concern, without doubting for a moment the correctness of this opinion.

And in no nation was this opinion more firmly fixed or more uniformly acted upon than by the English Government and English people. They not only seized them on the coast of Africa, and sold them or held them in slavery for their own use; but they took them as ordinary articles of merchandise to every country where they could make a profit on them, and were far more extensively engaged in this commerce than any other nation in the world."[4]

Judge Taney, the top Judge in America, had spoken. The law of the land was clear and undisputable. Black people were things, stripped of their humanity, reduced to nothing more than chattel; bought, sold, and discarded at the whim of white enslavers. Their bodies were commodities, their labor exploited, their pain ignored, all to fuel an insatiable machine of greed. The system did not merely tolerate their suffering, it thrived on it, legalizing and institutionalizing their bondage to ensure wealth and power remained concentrated in the hands of those who saw them as nothing more than property.

Slavery and mass incarceration remain functionally interchangeable beneath the shadow of the 13th Amendment, perpetuating a system that exploits and dehumanizes under the pretense of justice. This enduring framework forms the bedrock of our modern criminal legal system.

---

[4] Dred Scott, 60 U.S. at 407

Chapter Two – The Complicity of the Judiciary

The complicity of the judiciary in driving mass incarceration is often overlooked, with more attention directed toward sloppy policing, negligent detectives, unethical prosecutors, or ineffective defense attorneys. Yet the blame is far from one-sided because every corner of the justice system bears responsibility.

Some may argue that chattel slavery and incarceration are fundamentally different. Technically, that is true, the enslaved had no legal rights, while a prisoner had rights before he/she became a prisoner, including the right to a trial by jury, and if convicted, retain the possibility of freedom through appellate processes and post-conviction proceedings.

However, this comparison fails to consider the evolution of forced labor as society and technology have advanced. The reality is that slavery has adapted to fit modern structures. The enslaved no longer toil in open fields, but the same exploitative systems persist, now repurposed to operate within industries like the prison system. The setting has changed, but the control, coercion, and economic exploitation remain.

The limited rights afforded to incarcerated people remain at the mercy of a judiciary, whose potential complicity cannot be ignored. Most judges exhibit a predisposition against those branded "criminals," reinforcing systemic bias under the guise of legal neutrality.

The 13th Amendment's loophole was no accident. It was language crafted with intention, designed to preserve slavery under the sanitized guise of criminal justice. The amendment didn't abolish bondage; it renamed it. "*Except as punishment for a crime*" became the gateway for legal exploitation.

The courtroom is the new auction block.[5] Bodies are appraised by everything that happens in the courtroom. The chains and overseers are still there for those that remained detained and not released from custody prior to trial.

When profit shapes policy, captivity becomes currency. Corporations bankroll legislation that tightens the noose, and lawmakers will comply because they want to get re-elected. The prison pipeline grows, not because it works, but because it pays. And the bodies it consumes? Black, poor, over-surveilled. The system is not broken; it's bought. And the courtroom is not a temple of justice, it's an ATM.

The prison-industrial complex, fueled by profit and exploitation, turns inmates into a labor force, one that is undervalued, overworked, and often unpaid. Prisons are modern-day plantations, supplying cheap labor to industries that benefit from incarceration[6].

Beyond forced labor, the system itself is designed to perpetuate cycles

---

[5] Becky Little, "Does an Exception Clause in the 13th Amendment Still Permit Slavery?" History.com, October 2, 2018, updated May 28, 2025, https://www.history.com/articles/13th-amendment-slavery-loophole-jim-crow-prisons ; Nadia Alfadel Coloma, "Rethinking Prison Labor under the 13th Amendment," UChicago News, June 5, 2025, https://news.uchicago.edu/story/rethinking-prison-labor-under-13th-amendment

[6] Prison–industrial complex, Wikipedia, last modified 2025 (accessed Sep. 9, 2025), https://en.wikipedia.org/wiki/Prison%E2%80%93industrial_complex

of imprisonment, ensuring that those who enter it rarely escape its grasp. Harsh sentencing laws, discriminatory policing, and privatized prison industries work together to keep cells filled and the system thriving. The narrative of "justice" becomes a cover for sustained economic and social control.

The 2024 Annual Report from the National Registry of Exonerations confirms what communities have long known: wrongful convictions are not rare, they are racialized:

- In 2024, 147 people were exonerated for crimes they did not commit.
- Black individuals accounted for nearly 60% of those exonerations, despite making up only about 13% of the U.S. population.
- These exonerees lost an average of 13.5 years to wrongful imprisonment, totaling 1,980 years stolen.
- The report also found that official misconduct played a role in 71% of cases, and perjury or false accusations were present in 72%[7]

The racial disparity is undeniable. Black individuals are exonerated more frequently than any other group, not because of better legal advocacy, but because they are disproportionately wrongfully convicted. This reflects deep-rooted bias, woven into policing, prosecution, sentencing, and jury selection. The cases of Troy Davis

---

[7] *National Registry of Exonerations, 2024 Annual Report*, April 2, 2025, a project of the University of California Irvine Newkirk Center for Science & Society; University of Michigan Law School; Michigan State University College of Law, 2–3.

and Marcellus Williams are grim reminders: both men were executed despite compelling evidence of innocence.[8] Their deaths weren't just tragedies, they were indictments of a system more committed to closure than to truth.

This isn't just a flaw in the system, it's a pattern. A pattern that criminalizes Blackness, erodes trust, and devastates families. The unacceptable remains acceptable because this land has dehumanized Black bodies to the point that lynchings in broad daylight can be ruled as suicides without investigation.

The failure of the justice system is not just a matter of isolated mistakes, it's the result of widespread systemic negligence and corruption. Sloppy police work leads to botched investigations, lazy detectives overlook key evidence, prosecutors bend the truth to secure convictions, defense attorneys fail to provide the vigorous representation their clients deserve, and the judiciary goes along with it because it's all done in the name of the law.

The data from the National Registry of Exonerations 2024 Annual Report is both damning and illuminating:

---

[8] Ed Pilkington, "Troy Davis was executed despite serious doubts over his guilt," The Guardian, September 22, 2011; Joseph Ax and Brad Brooks, "Missouri executes Marcellus Williams despite pleas from prosecutor and victim's family," Reuters, September 25, 2024.

Top Contributing Factors to Wrongful Convictions in '24

Factor	**Number of Cases**	**Percent age**
Perjury or False Accusation	106	72%
Official Misconduct	104	71%
False or Misleading Forensic Evidence	42	29%
Ineffective Assistance of Counsel	48	33%
Mistaken Witness Identification	38	26%
False Confessions	22	15%

Most cases involved multiple forms of misconduct, including:

- Failure to disclose exculpatory evidence (95 cases)
- Witness tampering (43 cases)
- Perjury by officials (39 cases)
- Police misconduct during interrogations (9 cases)
- Prosecutorial dishonesty in court (8 cases)[9]

This data doesn't just expose flaws, it reveals a pattern; A system that criminalizes Blackness, rewards deception, and punishes poverty.

When all these factors collide, innocent lives are ruined, families are shattered, and trust in the system erodes. It's not just about a few bad actors; it's about an entire structure that enables wrongful convictions and mass incarceration.

The fight for justice demands accountability at every level, from the street to the courtroom. Real reform means challenging the system, demanding better standards, and ensuring that those entrusted with power use it for justice, not convenience or personal gain.

Judges are entrusted with the responsibility of fairness and impartiality, ensuring that their decisions are based on the law and the facts, not personal biases or political influences.

When fear sits in the judge's chambers, justice rarely leaves the courtroom. Politically pressured, indifferent, or willfully complicit, these arbiters of law uphold flawed verdicts not because they must,

---

[9] National Registry of Exonerations, Exonerations in 2024, April 2, 2025, accessed September 9, 2025, https://exonerationregistry.org/sites/exonerationregistry.org/files/documents/2024_Annual_Report.pdf

but because they choose silence over scrutiny. Rather than challenge systemic failure, they rubber-stamp injustice, allowing the machinery of mass incarceration to grind on unhindered. When this cycle repeats, day after day, week after week, month after month, year after year, it deepens the tragedy for the very communities surrounding the courthouse. Generations carry the weight of trauma as they walk through those doors, sit in those courtrooms, and relive the pain of systemic injustice. Across America, emotions spill into hallways while lawyers, court reporters, and staff look on, shaking their heads, witnesses to a ritual that has become heartbreakingly routine.

The reality is that most judges come from prosecutorial backgrounds, which can subtly, or overtly, shape their approach to cases.[10] Having spent years advocating for the government, some may lean toward law enforcement perspectives, favoring the prosecution over defendants. This bias, whether intentional or subconscious, can lead to harsh sentencing, dismissive attitudes toward defense arguments, and a reluctance to challenge prosecutorial misconduct.

The consequences are profound: wrongful convictions persist, sentencing disparities deepen, and true justice remains elusive. Without meaningful accountability, judicial bias can undermine the very foundation of fairness the system claims to uphold.

---

[10] Christopher M. Berryessa, Prosecuting from the Bench? Examining Sources of Pro-Prosecution Bias in Judges, Legal and Criminological Psychology 28, no. 1 (2023): 1–14

Reforming judicial selection, increasing oversight, and demanding transparency in rulings are essential steps toward ensuring that courts serve justice rather than simply reinforcing governmental authority.

These systemic failures don't happen in a vacuum. In a justice system that profits from prison labor, every misstep becomes a mile marker on a rail line to incarceration. And once onboard, the ride rarely circles back, opportunity narrows, and freedom becomes a distant exit.

Evidence is the cornerstone of every criminal case. Its collection, handling, and presentation determine whether justice is served or manipulated.

The trial court plays a critical role in shaping how the case unfolds. Their decisions on admissibility of evidence determine what the jury sees, and, just as importantly, what they don't see. This can drastically impact the verdict, especially if key evidence is excluded due to technicalities or legal maneuvering.

Ultimately, while the jury may render the final verdict, the judge steers the course of justice from the shadows. Through rulings, evidentiary decisions, and judicial instructions, judges shape the narrative presented in court and define how the law is to be understood and applied. When the bench sets the boundaries, the jury deliberates within a cage built by authority.

It's not just judges, prosecutors, defense attorneys, detectives and police officers, its lab technicians, evidence collectors, forensic analysts, children services and a host of others, who can influence outcomes in ways that sustain oppression rather than serve justice. A single falsified report, missing piece of evidence, collusion or unethical forensic practice can determine whether someone is convicted or set free.

And with the prison-industrial complex profiting off incarceration, there is an inherent incentive to keep prison labor functioning.[11] Wrongful convictions, excessive sentencing, and prison labor contracts ensure that modern slavery remains disguised as criminal punishment.

True justice requires accountability at every level, from the courtroom to the labs, from police stations to prison walls. Otherwise, the system will continue to reinforce the very exploitation it claims to have abolished.

The loophole in the 13th Amendment has allowed slavery to evolve, not vanish, through the machinery of mass incarceration.[12] This system thrives when bad actors occupy critical roles across policing, prosecution, legislation, and the judiciary. It is not just flawed; it is engineered to exploit. To dismantle this modern iteration of bondage, the loophole must be closed entirely. And the profits, squeezed from caged labor and corporate contracts, must be pruned from the prison industrial complex at its root.

---

[11] American Civil Liberties Union, "Describing Modern Day Prison Labor's Roots in Slavery", press release, October 12, 2023.

[12] Innocence Project, How the 13th Amendment Kept Slavery Alive: Perspectives From the Prison Where Slavery Never Ended, September 17, 2021, accessed [insert your access date], https://innocenceproject.org/news/how-the-13th-amendment-kept-slavery-alive-perspectives-from-the-prison-where-slavery-never-ended/

Chapter Three - Power Moves

Power structures are determined to preserve its dominance and maintain the status quo. This behavior should come as no surprise, as individuals routinely engage in these actions. This dynamic transcends all groups; Black people practice this same behavior within its communities.

Whenever people gather, power structures begin to form. And too often, those who ascend to power do whatever it takes to maintain control, regardless of the setting, the scale, or the souls involved. These actions stem from selfish ambition, and James 3:14 makes it plain: such ambition is evil. Without repentance, this posture does not just miss the mark, it mirrors the spirit of the anti-Christ. It is un-Christian in nature, anti-kingdom in essence, and deeply destructive in practice.

The "United States of America" is not now and has never been a "Christian" nation. The Constitution never mentions Christianity. The First Amendment was not written to protect religion in government, it was written to protect government from religion.[13] Claims to the contrary come from wolves in sheep's clothing, cloaked in collective hypocrisy and wielding coded rhetoric to cling to power, all under the guise of Christianity.

The same power structures that crucified Jesus later distorted His image, transforming a dark-skinned Middle Eastern man into a

---

[13] "Treaty of Tripoli," signed June 7, 1797, United States Senate, Article 11, in First Amendment Encyclopedia, accessed September 9, 2025.
U.S. Constitution, Article VI, Clause 3.
Library of Congress, "Religion and the Federal Government, Part 1," Library of Congress, September 9, 2025.

blonde-haired, blue-eyed American icon.[14] In doing so, they turned the Messiah into a false idol, one crafted to affirm cultural dominance rather than reflect divine truth.

Some have carelessly claimed that it doesn't matter what Jesus looked like. But it absolutely does. Jesus was not an abstract idea. He was a real man who walked this earth, lived in a specific time, and existed in the historical record. He had a body. He had an appearance. To say His physical identity doesn't matter is to erase His humanity and to deny that He came in the flesh.

Christianity is not the "White man's religion." That's a colonizer's myth, not a historical fact. Christianity's roots reach deep into the African continent, long before European empires ever claimed it.[15] In Acts 8:30, the Apostle Philip engages with an Ethiopian official, an early convert who was reading from the Book of Isaiah. Africa didn't borrow Christianity; it helped to shape it.

The Whitewashed image of Jesus wasn't accidental, it was strategic. It allowed Christianity to be co-opted by systems of white supremacy, turning the Savior into a symbol of dominance instead of deliverance. [16]That image became an idol, sanctifying power structures that enslaved, segregated, and subjugated. It erased the dark-skinned,

---

[14] Robyn J. Whitaker, "Jesus Wasn't White: He Was a Brown-Skinned, Middle Eastern Jew. Here's Why That Matters," The Conversation (blog), March 29, 2018, republished as "Jesus wasn't white: he was a brown-skinned, Middle Eastern Jew. Here's why that matters," ABC News, March 30, 2018, https://www.abc.net.au/news/2018-03-29/jesus-wasnt-white-he-was-a-brown-skinned-jew/9600402

[15] Andrew Butterworth, "African Christianity Thrived, Long Before White Men Arrived," The Gospel Coalition, November 16, 2022, accessed September 9, 2025, https://africa.thegospelcoalition.org/article/african-christianity-thrived-long-before-white-men-arrived/

[16] Gafney, Wil. "White Supremacy In the Church." Wil Gafney's Blog, March 10, 2016. https://www.wilgafney.com/2016/03/10/white-supremacy-in-the-church/

Middle Eastern rabbi from Nazareth and replaced Him with a figure who could sit comfortably atop empires.

It's a false image, crafted, consecrated, and stamped into the hearts and minds of Black people for generations. So deeply ingrained that many refuse to see the lie. It has become tradition. Reverence. Identity. But it is idolatry masked as faith. And when a lie is worshiped long enough, it starts to feel like the truth.

God forbids idolatry. God warned us,

"Therefore watch yourselves very carefully, so that you do not become corrupt and make for yourselves an idol, an image of any shape, whether formed like a man or a woman[.]"

- *Deuteronomy 4:15-16*

Black people need Jesus, not the whitewashed image crafted by the empire, but the living Word of God. Through Christ, our communities have endured slavery, segregation, surveillance, and scorn. And yet we rise. Not because oppression relented, but because grace remained. From hush harbors (plantations) to pulpits, from prison cells to protest marches, we have drawn strength from the One who was despised and rejected, wounded and yet triumphant. Our help has always come from the Lord, and our faith has always been an act of holy resistance.

(Our faith must) never hinge on what others think or say about us. Our dignity doesn't require approval, nor does it depend on the gaze of any other group or individual. When anyone engages with Black people only to provoke, distract, or diminish, their ire is not about us, it's about them. Their nonstop comments reveals a wounded ego that manifests as rage, which comes from their own deep seated sense of inferiority that borders on obsession. They keep talking about Black people because we remind them that we survived despite the concerted efforts to destroy our existence. They simply cannot comprehend how we have survived and remain undefeated in many ways. They refuse to see God in us.

Black Americans survive with God and suffer without God. We are a unique nation, a people that are uniquely different from any other people in the Universe. Unfortunately, we have been desperately trying to fit in with other groups to our detriment. This is not to say that we should not engage or interact with other groups, of course we should. Black Americans, collectively, need to recognize its strength and character and learn to lovc and respect each other.

It should not matter what other people think about us or say about us or to us. It's better to maintain our dignity than to engage with anyone that is only seeking our attention and engagement from us. Any person that tries to engage this way with Black people feels inferior to Black people. That's why they are angry.

They look for ways to feed the machine of how media outlets portray us. It serves their inferiority complex and makes them feel better about themselves.

Black Americans are resilient. We are not defined by the chains that tried to bind us, but by the strength with which we broke them. Our story is not just one of suffering, it is one of triumph over it. We rose from the struggle of slavery, and in that rising, we became a testament to enduring power.

The rise from the ashes of slavery was driven by the desire to have a voice in who holds power over our daily existence in America, and to gain some control over our destiny in the country that our ancestors built. This would have never been a great nation without their labor, sacrifice, pain, blood, sweat and tears, and everyone knows it, even if they refuse to acknowledge it.

The ancestors labored relentlessly, building the wealth of a nation that gave them nothing in return, an injustice that stands in brutal contradiction to the Israelites, who did not leave Egypt empty-handed. In Exodus Chapter 12, when they were finally freed, they left with silver and gold, plundering their oppressors as a form of divine justice. Yet, in America, the builders of its prosperity, the enslaved, were denied even the smallest reparation for generations of stolen labor.

That is why Black Americans fight relentlessly for justice, because the struggle is not confined to the past. It lives on. It's like a victim forced to share space with their oppressor, every moment a reminder that freedom without equity is merely survival. The same systems that once sanctioned chains now deploy subtler tools; policy, propaganda, and dog whistles to uphold power.

This is the soil from which the Southern Strategy emerged: a calculated political maneuver designed to exploit racial tension, shift party allegiances, and fracture the promise of equal representation.[17] It rebranded oppression in the language of tradition, morality, and law and order, turning Black resilience into a threat and white fear into votes.

Scripture reminds us:

"Woe to those who make unjust laws, to those who issue oppressive decrees, to deprive the poor of their rights..."

\- *Isaiah 10:1–2*

This is more than history, it's prophecy. And it demands that Black Americans be not only aware, but fully awake.

This awakening echoes that night in Gethsemane. While Jesus was grieved to the point of death, praying alone in agony, His closest companions were asleep, unaware of the weight of what was

---

[17] Joseph A. Aistrup, The Southern Strategy Revisited: Republican Top-Down Advancement in the South (Lexington: University Press of Kentucky, 1996).

unfolding. Jesus asked them to keep watch, but they couldn't stay awake. And today, the world is much the same: injustice moves during the day, but people can't see it because they are sleeping.

To awaken is to reject complacency. It is to rise while others slumber, to pray while others protest their innocence through silence. The Gethsemane moment wasn't just about betrayal, it was about spiritual readiness. And this generation, like the disciples, must be shaken from slumber to recognize the hour and respond to it.

Just as Jesus prayed in agony at Gethsemane, betrayed not only by enemies but by the silence of sleeping friends, we stand in our own Gethsemane moment. The soul of the nation trembles under the weight of injustice, and still, too many are asleep, lulled by convenience, distracted by comfort, numb to suffering.

And while some slept, power whispered. The Southern Strategy crept in like Judas in the garden, quiet, strategic, deliberate. It reshaped political discourse, turning racial fear into votes, wrapping moral decay in religious language. It weaponized the pulpit and disguised oppression as tradition.

But the call of Christ at Gethsemane still echoes:

"Could you not watch with me one hour?"

- *Matthew 26:40*

Watching is not passive, it's prophetic. To stay awake is to resist. It is to expose the betrayal of justice masked by prayer, the policies that claim Christ while crucifying His truth.

Isaiah said it best:

"Awake, awake, put on strength... shake yourself from the dust!"

- *Isaiah 52:1–2*

This is the hour to awaken, not just in spirit, but in purpose. Because just as the cross followed the garden, consequence follows silence. And our refusal to sleep is how we reclaim the narrative.

Chapter Four – Black Americans

From the very beginning, Black Americans were forced to the margins, pressed down by a system built to exclude them.[1][4][5] The oppression wasn't accidental; it was deliberate, calculated, and relentless. [2][3] Every barrier, every policy, every injustice was crafted to keep them subdued. [6][9] Opportunities were withheld, progress was sabotaged, and a cycle of struggle was engineered to remain unbroken. [2][3] This wasn't just neglect, it was design. And that design bore the signature of law. [4][5][6]

This form of sabotage is not broad, it's precise, surgically inflicted on Black Americans alone. [2][3] Not Black immigrants who arrived by choice or circumstance, but the descendants of those who were enslaved in this land. [7][8] This is a unique legacy of injustice, rooted in stolen labor and perpetuated by denial. [4][5][6]

There is an outstanding debt, incalculable and unpaid, that America has owed since emancipation. [7][8][9] A debt not diluted across diasporas but singularly held by the lineage born in bondage. [7][8] That burden is more than symbolic; it is structural, generational, and crushing. [10][11][16] It is the weight that clips wings before flight, the silent force that stifles upward motion in the so-called land of the free.[2][3][10]

From the founding of this nation, Black Americans were thrust into a system that never intended to acknowledge their full humanity. [4][5] The laws were clear, and so was their purpose: to justify slavery, to normalize exclusion, and to perpetuate a hierarchy where Blackness equated to inferiority. [4][5][6]

The aftermath of emancipation did not bring repair. Post-Reconstruction and the Compromise of 1877 brought new forms of bondage: Jim Crow laws, convict leasing, redlining, police brutality, disenfranchisement. [2][3][9][14][15] Each policy meticulously designed to contain Black progress, to keep it from flourishing or even budding. [2][3][9] The sabotage was not indiscriminate; it was precise and unrepentant, inflicted upon the descendants of the enslaved as if their existence alone were an indictment of the past. [2][3][14] They bore the weight of history's shame, punished for refusing to disappear. [10][11]

Immigrants of African descent arrive and encounter racism, yes, but they were not born under the shadow of an unpaid debt. [7][8] That debt is owed to Black Americans alone. [7][8] It's inherited like a last name, passed down like a scar, and carried like a weight strapped to the spine of every generation. [10][11][16]

And while the slogan says, "justice for all," the machinery of the law exposes that promise as a lie. [12][13][15] Time and again, justice has been withheld from those who built this nation, and to their legacy. [12][13][15]

Legacies of inequity aren't incidental, they are deliberate. [2][3][9] They have been sustained across generations through calculated legislation and complicit silence. [4][5][6][17] This architecture of exclusion has not merely shaped America; it has built it. [2][3][9]

To understand Black struggle is to understand policy. [2][3][9 To understand resistance is to understand that even against an empire of suppression, Black Americans have never stopped reaching upward, demanding truth, and reclaiming the dignity that was systematically stripped away. [12][13][16]

The call to "move on" echoes through history like a refrain designed to erase it. [10][11] But Black Americans will not move on, because we were never meant to forget. [10][11] The blood of our ancestors still cries out from the soil, and their work remains unfinished. [7][8] To move on without reckoning is to betray the memory, the mission, and the mantle they left behind. [7][8][16]

Forgiveness cannot exist without accountability. [8][9] Forgetting, in the absence of justice, becomes a tool, one that shields the oppressor and silences the oppressed. [8][9][17] Forgive and forget is possible when justice is done and accountability is real. [8][9]

To forgive without atonement is to permit repetition. [8][9] To forget without repair is to grant impunity. [8][9][16]

This is not just about what was done, it's about what continues. [2][3][9][12][13][15] The debt is not theoretical, and the pain isn't archived. [7][8][10][11] Black Americans have never had the luxury of forgetting, because the consequences of that legacy are alive in every institution, every disparity, every act of sanctioned neglect. [2][3][9][12][13][15]

When injustice persists unacknowledged, any call for forgiveness becomes complicit in the harm. [8][9][17] The moral ledger remains unsettled, and the law itself, when wielded without conscience, becomes complicit too. [4][5][6][17]

If you didn't know, Black Americans have been making noise for a long time. [12][13][16] Not the kind that fades into background static, but the kind that shakes foundations. [12][13][16] Our noise is a refusal. A resistance. A reminder. [12][13][16] It says: if we have to be uncomfortable, so do you. [16][17] If we must carry the weight of history, then you must feel its pressure too. [10][11][16] This noise is not rage without reason, it is the sound of unfinished justice, of ancestors who still speak, of systems that still bleed. [12][13][16] And we will not be silenced. [12][13][16]

Not all Black Americans think alike. [16][17] We are not a monolith, we are a mosaic. [16][17] But within that mosaic, there are those who will bend over backwards to preserve white comfort, even at the cost of their own dignity. [16][17] Whether out of survival, strategy, or internalized narratives, some have learned to silence their truth so others can sleep soundly. [16][17] But comfort is not the goal, justice is. [8][9][16] And justice will never be birthed in silence. [12][13][16]

This dichotomy creates a quiet war within the Black community [16][17] It is not just ideological, it's spiritual, generational, and deeply personal. [10][11][16] The irony is striking: the primary tension among Black Americans often centers not on Black liberation, but on white comfortability. [16][17] One side demands truth, even if it disrupts the room. [16][17] The other side polices tone, fearing that discomfort will cost us access, opportunity, or safety. [16][17] But comfort has never been the measure of justice. [8][9][16] And unity built on silence is not unity, it is surrender. [16][17]

This is, of course, a carryover from slavery, when survival depended on appeasement, and safety was often purchased through silence. [10][11][14] The legacy of that trauma still lingers, tempting some to prioritize white comfort over Black truth. [10][11][16][17] But that temptation is not benign. It is corrosive. [10][11] It teaches us to shrink, to soften, to self-edit in the presence of power. [16][17] And that is spiritually, psychologically, and politically unhealthy for Black Americans. [10][11][16] Comfort has never been a path to liberation. [8][9][16] Only truth has the power to set people free. [8][9][12][13][16]

References

[1] Williams, I. (2022). Black bodies in America as the metaphors for oppression, poverty, violence, and hate: Searching for sustainable solutions beyond the black-letter law. Journal of Black Studies, 53(4), 291-318. https://doi.org/10.1177/00219347221074060

[2] Althoff, L., & Reichardt, H. (2024). Jim Crow and black economic progress after slavery. Quarterly Journal of Economics, 139(3), 1785-1850. https://doi.org/10.1093/qje/qjae023

[3] Bailey, C. M. (2022). The evolution of anti-blackness in the American South: How slavery and segregation perpetuates the victimization of black people. Journal of Research in Crime and Delinquency, 60(2), 147-182. https://doi.org/10.1177/00224278221120811

[4] Perea, J. F. (2012). Race and constitutional law casebooks: Recognizing the proslavery Constitution. Michigan Law Review, 110(6), 1017-1056.

[5] Edwards, L. F. (2007). Status without rights: African Americans and the tangled history of law and governance in the nineteenth-century U.S. South. The American Historical Review, 112(2), 365-393. https://doi.org/10.1086/AHR.112.2.365

[6] Wahl, J. B. (1996). American slavery and the path of the law. Social Science History, 20(1), 1-40. https://doi.org/10.1017/S0145553200021635

[7] Martin, M. T., Yaquinto, M., Lyons, D., & Brown, M. K. (Eds.). (2007). Redress for historical injustices in the United States: On reparations for slavery, Jim Crow, and their legacies. Duke University Press. https://doi.org/10.1215/9780822389811

[8] Ford, A. L. (2018). The influence of reparations internalized oppression and racial centrality across systemic and psychological factors concerning the African American community. Social Work and Business Journal, 1(1), Article 3. https://digitalcommons.pepperdine.edu/swbj/vol1/iss1/3/

[9] Remedying the health implications of structural racism through reparations. (2022). George Washington Law Review, 90(4), 1018-1076.

[10] Sweeting, A., Akinyemi, E., & Holman, D. M. (2022). Parental preconception adversity and offspring health in African Americans: A systematic review of intergenerational studies. Trauma, Violence, & Abuse, 24(4), 2547-2565. https://doi.org/10.1177/15248380221074320

[11] Graff, G. (2018). The intergenerational trauma of slavery and its aftermath. Journal of Psychohistory, 45(3), 162-183.

[12] Hutto, J. W., & Green, R. D. (2016). Social movements against racist police brutality and Department of Justice intervention in Prince George's County, Maryland. Journal of Urban Health, 93(1), 89-121. https://doi.org/10.1007/S11524-015-0013-X

[13] Kahfi, M. (2023). Review of Clarence Taylor, Fight the Power: African Americans and the long history of police brutality in New York City. The American Historical Review, 128(2), 847-849. https://doi.org/10.1093/ahr/rhad114

[14] Carter, E. (2023). Review of Silvan Niedermeier, The Color of the Third Degree: Racism, Police Torture, and Civil Rights in the American South, 1930–1955. The American Historical Review, 128(1), 373-374. https://doi.org/10.1093/ahr/rhac401

[15] King, B. A., & Erickson, L. (2016). Disenfranchising the enfranchised: Exploring the relationship between felony disenfranchisement and African American voter turnout. Journal of Black Studies, 47(8), 799-821. https://doi.org/10.1177/0021934716659195

[16] Yadon, N. (2022). "They say we're violent": The multidimensionality of race in perceptions of police brutality and BLM. Perspectives on Politics, 20(4), 1331-1349. https://doi.org/10.1017/S1537592722001013

[17] Gooden, S. T. (2015). Race and social equity: A nervous area of government. Routledge. https://doi.org/10.4324/9781315701301

Chapter Five – Check, Not Checkmate

Black Americans woke up a long time ago and have been making a whole lot of noise since then. We shouted in the streets, marched in the rain, and raised our voices in protest and in pain. We have rioted when ignored, preached when dismissed, and kept pressing forward with a continual chip on our shoulder, not out of bitterness, but born from centuries of betrayal. Our stance has never been silent; it has been a mirror held to power, demanding it confront the error of its ways.

But we have not always been spiritually awake. There have been seasons where weariness overtook watchfulness, where trauma numbed the prophetic voice. In some moments, survival became the priority, leaving little room to interrogate the spiritual implications of injustice. We marched while mourning, spoke truth with trembling mouths, and prayed through pain. But even in our slumber, God whispered, stirred, and called us back to the mountain. Because awakening is not a once-for-all moment, it is a continual return to truth.

Historically, Black Americans have recognized that voting power is not just a constitutional right but a tool for liberation. Understanding its crucial importance, Black Americans fought relentlessly, enduring violence, intimidation, and systemic suppression, until victory was secured with the passage of the Voting Rights Act of 1965, a hard-won triumph in the ongoing battle for justice and equality.[18]

---

[18] Lawson, Steven F. Black Ballots: Voting Rights in the South, 1944–1969. Columbia

But that hard-fought victory came at a price, as those in power never surrender control without a plan of attack. Revenge is real. The right to vote was more than a legal win, it was a seismic shift in the balance of power.[19] And for such a profound transformation, there had to be consequences. The backlash was swift, ruthless, and calculated, a desperate attempt to undermine, suppress, and claw back the power that Black Americans had rightfully claimed.

Those in power play chess, strategizing moves well in advance, anticipating opposition, and ensuring their control remains intact. Meanwhile, those struggling at the bottom play checkers, often viewing victories as the destination rather than just another step in an ongoing fight. They celebrate wins like a lean across a finish line, unaware that the match is far from over and that those in power were already plotting their next move to maintain domination and control.

When Black Americans secured the right to vote, propelled by an unstoppable spiritual force, they exhaled, believing they had crossed a threshold into a new era of freedom. At that moment, our guard was down. That is when those in power fully exploited the loophole in the 13th Amendment possible.

While U.S. combat troops were entrenched in the Vietnam War overseas, another battle was being waged at home. On June 16, 1971, Richard Nixon officially declared the War on Drugs, branding drug

---

University Press, 1999.

[19] McAdam, Doug. Political Process and the Development of Black Insurgency, 1930–1970. University of Chicago Press, 1982.

use as "public enemy #1." [20] This declaration was made during the overwhelming media coverage of the anti-war protests and urban uprisings, setting the stage for a policy that would disproportionately target Black communities and fuel decades of systemic oppression under the guise of crime prevention.

After declaring the War on Drugs, President Nixon established the Drug Enforcement Administration (DEA) in 1973, marking a shift from public health strategies to aggressive policing. [21] The move laid the infrastructure for a carceral approach to drug use, one that criminalized addiction rather than treated it. Yet the crack epidemic did not emerge until 1981, under President Reagan's administration, which took Nixon's framework and supercharged it with mandatory minimums.

Between racialized media campaigns, and sweeping federal interventions, what began as a political maneuver metastasized into a national punishment strategy. A punishment strategy that disproportionately devastated Black communities across this nation.

Reagan's trickle-down economics was a catastrophe for working-class families, particularly in urban centers. As tax breaks funneled wealth upward, corporations cut costs by shuttering local operations or relocating overseas, gutting communities and eroding job security. Trickle-down economics prioritized shareholders over workers and profits over people, treating labor as expendable and neighborhoods

---

[20] Baum, Dan. Smoke and Mirrors: The War on Drugs and the Politics of Failure. Little, Brown, 1996.

[21] Drug Enforcement Administration, "DEA History," U.S. Department of Justice.

as collateral damage. What was sold as economic uplift became a blueprint for inequality and poverty.

Poverty is not born from the selfishness and greediness of those in power. Yet when ignorant people gaze upon the ugliness of poverty, they do not indict the architects, the systems, the policies, the profiteers of poverty, the powerful people. Instead, they condemn the poor for being poor, the broken for being broken, and the ugly for daring to be seen.

With unemployment soaring, President Ronald Reagan signed the Anti-Drug Abuse Act of 1986, allocating $1.7 billion to escalate the war on drugs.[22] The legislation introduced mandatory minimums for drug offenses, fueling a surge in incarceration and deepening racial disparities in sentencing. It was not a partisan project, it was a bipartisan endorsement of punitive policy, co-sponsored by both Republicans and Democrats, including then-Senator Joe Biden. The result? Decades of devastation, disproportionately borne by Black and Brown communities.

In a 1994 interview cited by journalist Dan Baum and later reported by the [Equal Justice Initiative][23], John Ehrlichman, Nixon's former domestic policy chief, laid bare the true intent behind the War on Drugs.[24]

---

[22] Anti-Drug Abuse Act of 1986, Pub.L. 99–570 and Tonry, Michael. Malign Neglect: Race, Crime, and Punishment in America. Oxford University Press, 1995.

[23] https://eji.org/news/nixon-war-on-drugs-designed-to-criminalize-black-people/

[24] Baum, Dan. "Legalize It All." Harper's Magazine, April 2016 and Equal Justice Initiative, "The War on Drugs," eji.org.

He stated:

"The Nixon campaign in 1968, and the Nixon White House after that, had two enemies: the antiwar left and Black people... We knew we couldn't make it illegal to be either against the war or Black, but by getting the public to associate the hippies with marijuana and Blacks with heroin, and then criminalizing both heavily, we could disrupt those communities... Did we know we were lying about the drugs? Of course we did."

This was no mere policy failure, it was a calculated strategy of racial and political suppression. The War on Drugs functioned as a tool to vilify, destabilize, and incarcerate Black and Brown communities under the false banner of public safety. Its legacy reverberates still: in sentencing disparities, in the relentless over-policing of marginalized neighborhoods, and in the machinery of mass incarceration that continues to grind lives into silence.

The War on Drugs has ravaged Black communities nationwide, leaving destruction in its wake. It continues to tear apart Black families, its impact cascading through generations like a relentless tide. Instead of fostering generational wealth, it has perpetuated generational trauma, trapping communities in cycles of loss, incarceration, and systemic oppression.

No sum of money can atone for the psychological warfare waged against every Black soul born, raised, educated, and surviving on this soil. This is not merely trauma, it is a calculated assault on identity, dignity, and peace. And it is ongoing.

No amount of atonement offered will be sufficient. No amount of money, apology or reform can undo the damage. Because the wound is not merely historical; it is present, pulsing, and perpetuated. Atonement must begin, but it must never presume to finish.

Atonement is not a transaction; it is a moral reckoning. It is essential not only for those who were harmed, but also for those who caused harm, and for their descendants. Atonement restores the dignity of the wounded, and their descendants, but it also rescues the souls of the ones who cause harm.

Without atonement, the perpetrators and their heirs remain trapped in a false innocence, clinging to a hollow high ground built on denial and unexamined privilege. They may hold power and/or privilege, but they forfeit integrity. They may escape accountability, but they cannot escape the erosion of their own moral standing. Some may amass wealth in this world; they will inherit no treasures in the next. Their voices will echo from the abyss, a haunting reminder that justice cannot be bought.

Chief Justice Taney may be long gone, but his legacy was never laid to rest; it was embalmed, exalted, and passed down as doctrine. This spirit lives not in graveyards but in law books, in courtrooms where justice is still a privilege of whiteness, and in policies that codify suffering while cloaking it as order.

The *Dred Scott* decision is not historical residue; it's a living blueprint. The same machinery that upheld slavery now sustains mass incarceration, selective police enforcement, and racialized economic exploitation. [25] It operates with a grin, naming oppression "justice," stamping inequality with "procedure," and treating Black pain as background noise.

Implicit bias is its camouflage, but power is its engine. And when truth stares it down, it blinks without shame. America struts in high heels, seduced by profit and willing to sell its soul for the highest bidder.

If you refuse to see the Spirit of Dred Scott in our "justice system," it's not because it's hidden, it's because you've chosen blindness over truth. God calls upon humanity to seek truth:[26] Isaiah 5:20, warns, "*Woe to those who call evil good and good evil, who put darkness for light and light for darkness*."

The War on Drugs strengthened police forces, granting them unchecked power to disproportionately target and over-police Black communities. [27] Instead of enforcing laws equitably, they weaponize them, applying harsh penalties in Black neighborhoods while turning a blind eye elsewhere. This deliberate imbalance ensures that slavery, though rebranded under new disguises, persists for Black Americans.

The *Dred Scott* decision is more than a ghost, it is a shadow cast across centuries, still alive and doing remarkably well in modern America. This nation, shaped by slavery, sanctioned by *Dred Scott*,

---

[25] Blackmon, Douglas A. Slavery by Another Name: The Re-Enslavement of Black Americans from the Civil War to World War II. Anchor Books, 2008.

[26] Stevenson, Bryan. Just Mercy: A Story of Justice and Redemption. Spiegel & Grau, 2014

[27] Hinton, Elizabeth. From the War on Poverty to the War on Crime: The Making of Mass Incarceration in America. Harvard University Press, 2016.

and calcified through the policies of the War on Drugs, has consistently chosen injustice over accountability. It has refused the morally righteous path, denying Black Americans, born here, raised here, buried here, the restitution that was earned.

And whether direct victims or survivors of systems meticulously engineered to oppress and erase, Black communities have endured generational harm without meaningful redress. The instruments of exploitation simply evolve: new disguises, same devastation.

Chapter Six – A Spiritual War

Dred Scott was decided in the name of the law, but never in the name of justice. [28] There was no room for it. The God we serve, however, does not worship law. God loves justice. [29]And if this system dares to call itself just, then its decisions must be rendered not in the name of precedent, not in the name of power, but in the name of justice.

But let us be clear, this long fight has been more than political dysfunction or judicial failure. This has been a spiritual war.[30]

Our struggle is not against flesh and blood, our struggle is against the authorities and against the powers of this dark world and against the spiritual forces of evil in the heavenly realms. Ephesians 6:12

Because this is a spiritual war, true victory will not be found in court filings, marches, or economic resistance. Those are tools, but they are not the sword.

This battle transcends the physical and political; it is fought in the unseen, waged in the soul of the nation itself.

And it will only be won wearing the Full Armor of God utilizing the spiritual weapons for offense and defense. Ephesians 6:10-18.

---

[28] Cohen, J. E. (1963). The Dred Scott Decision: Historical and Legal Analysis of Injustice in 19th-Century America. Harvard Law Review, 76(4), 653–675.

[29] Bell, Derrick. (2008). Race, Racism, and American Law (6th ed.). Aspen Publishers.

[30] Cone, James H. (2011). The Cross and the Lynching Tree. Orbis Books.

The Armor of God: Spiritual Weapons for Warfare

Weapon	Spiritual Function
Belt of Truth	Grounds you in honesty, integrity, and the unshakable truth of God's Word.
Breastplate of Righteousness	Guards your heart with the righteousness of Christ, protects against guilt and accusation.
Shoes of the Gospel of Peace	Anchors your steps in readiness and peace, empowering you to move with purpose and grace.
Shield of Faith	Deflects the fiery darts of doubt, fear, and deception, faith is your active defense.
Helmet of Salvation	Covers your mind with assurance, clarity, and identity in Christ.
Sword of the Spirit	The Word of God, your only offensive weapon, sharp enough to cut through lies and darkness.
Prayer (v.18)	The power source; activates and sustains every other weapon. It's how you stay connected to divine strategy.

Our resistance must be anchored in more than earthly systems; it must draw power from divine strength. Only when we stand in sacred alignment will justice not just be pursued but prevail.

This battle is spiritual, not tribal. The enemy does not care about skin color; he thrives on division, deception, and unrepented sin. Those who refuse to atone, regardless of their heritage, align themselves with darkness. And those who harbor hatred in their hearts, on either side, stand with Satan, not with God.

The Rev. Dr. Martin Luther King, Jr. was clear: He didn't hate white people. Hate is surrendering to the enemy. The temptation to hate must be rejected through spiritual warfare. Dr. King said, "Hate cannot drive out hate; only love can do that."

If anyone has hate in their heart, let them uproot it. Not with denial, but with deliberate love. Refocus your attention: not on what you think you hate, but on what you are called to love, because hatred is a distraction from purpose. It clouds judgment, corrodes compassion.

Satan hates all humans. He does not discriminate. So, there is a critical shift that must be acknowledged: while the War on Drugs was originally designed to disproportionately target Black Americans, it has since spread like an unchecked wildfire. Today, its reach extends beyond race alone, ensnaring communities of all backgrounds in a system that thrives on exploitation, criminalization, and control.[31]

---

[31] Rosenberg, Alana, et al. (2015). "Comparing Black and White Drug Offenders: Implications for Racial Disparities in Criminal Justice and Reentry Policy and

The catastrophic impact of the War on Drugs has spread far beyond urban centers, engulfing rural communities in its wake. These areas, once overlooked, now suffer the same relentless cycles of poverty, incarceration, and systemic devastation. And with the rise of fentanyl, the crisis has transcended race and geography, proving that destruction also does not discriminate.

As the War on Drugs has expanded beyond its original, racially targeted framework, the response to substance abuse has shifted in an unequal manner. When drugs wear a Black face, defendants are often criminalized, framed as a moral failing that demands punishment. But when drugs wear a white face, the narrative transforms into one of addiction, deserving compassion and rehabilitation.

The War on Drugs was never just policy, it was a machine. Engineered by racism, powered by greed, and calibrated to devastate Black communities [32] across this nation. It criminalized pain, punished poverty, and turned neighborhoods into battlegrounds. But the Black American spirit will survive, the way it has survived every demonic weapon employed against it.

Black Americans were not merely slave laborers, they were spiritual warriors. On cotton fields and sugar plantations, their hands bore the weight of empire, but their spirits bore the weight of glory. They praised through pain, prayed through persecution, and prophesied

---

Programming." Substance Use & Misuse, 50(13), 1761–1770. https://doi.org/10.3109/10826084.2015.1036485

[32] Alexander, Michelle. (2010). The New Jim Crow: Mass Incarceration in the Age of Colorblindness. The New Press.

through song. Every moan was a message. Every hymn, a hidden map to freedom. They didn't just endure, they consecrated the soil with faith, turning sites of bondage into sanctuaries of hope.

Resilient beyond measure, unstoppable in pursuit, and unwavering in the face of generational adversity. For every attempt to silence our voice, we raised it higher. When justice ran dry, we marched, we sang, we fought, and we did not fold.

Despite the crushing weight of institutional sabotage, we claimed the unclaimed. Through bloodshed in Selma, fire in Birmingham, and defiance across centuries, Black Americans won the right to vote, not because it was freely given, but because we made it undeniable. That right wasn't granted. It was seized. Earned. Paid for with courage.

Our fight for justice is ongoing, but never in vain. Every protest, every ballot, every act of survival is a line written in history, proof that no amount of oppression can extinguish a people who have turned resistance into legacy.

Imagine generations watching the rise of a man whose very existence defied the architecture of exclusion. When Barack Obama was elected President in 2008 and re-elected in 2012, Black Americans didn't just claim the White House, we shattered every ceiling designed to be impenetrable.

That moment echoed far beyond ballots. It was the voice of our ancestors finally heard through the thunder of progress. It was proof that no barrier, no law, no prejudice, no silence, was ever permanent.

Black Americans, forged in the furnace of struggle, had not only survived the storm. They had rewritten its forecast.

The symbolism was colossal: a family that could've been owned in America now owned its highest office. And while that achievement didn't erase injustice, it showed the boundlessness of possibility when resilience meets resolve.

Black Americans have shattered ceilings, redefined industries, and transformed this nation, leading in politics and law, business and entrepreneurship, science and technology, medicine, arts and entertainment, sports and beyond. Every victory is hard-won, but none have ever been beyond our reach.

We build. We innovate. We rise. And we will keep rising.

Black Americans have contributed to advancements in education, manufacturing, military service, and beyond.

The achievements of Black Americans are a testament to resilience, creativity, and excellence despite systemic challenges.

Black Americans continue to rise in the face of relentless oppression, not because the system lifts us, but because God sustains us.

Yes, we are living in the backlash, the tremors that follow when power is disrupted and truth is spoken from the highest office in the land. The election of a Black American president cracked the foundation of a carefully constructed narrative, and the system responded with fury. Voter suppression, judicial rollbacks, and legislative sabotage are all part of the counterattack. We are in Check. The king has been cornered. But this is not Checkmate. Because the board is still active, the pieces are still moving, and the spirit of our ancestors still whispers strategy. We are not out of moves, we are just being called to play with precision, with unity, and with prophetic boldness.

Psalm 103:6 declares, *"The Lord works righteousness and justice for all the oppressed."* That truth is our anchor. Our survival is not accidental, it is spiritual. Our resistance is not just cultural, it is sacred.

America's greatness cannot be declared, it must be proven. And proof requires reckoning. Centuries of unpaid labor were not simply an economic theft; they were a spiritual violation. The sweat and blood of our ancestors built the bones of this nation, brick by stolen brick. And that debt has not been settled.

Reparations aren't just a policy debate, they are a moral imperative. What was taken must be returned. What was broken must be healed. Until America confronts the cost of its prosperity, until it acknowledges that the freedom it boasts was built on bondage, its claim to greatness will remain hollow, and will never be fulfilled.

The spiritual principle is clear: you cannot feast on the fruit and forsake the hands that labored for the harvest. Justice may be delayed, but it is never erased because heaven knows everything.

The universe was spoken into existence by the voice of God. It does not bend to judicial loopholes or legal fictions; it moves according to spiritual principles.

Let's use a different context as an example. In this fallen system, human judges have ruled that deception is permissible by law enforcement officers when interrogating a suspect because it could lead to a confession. They call it strategy. Heaven calls it sin. When an officer places worldly judgments above God's judgment, or when truth is elevated above lies, neither the officer nor the judge is upholding justice. Both are selling their souls. Because justice without truth is not justicc at all, it is manipulation with a badge and dressed in a black robe.

In the same manner, reparations are not merely a legal or judicial issue; it is also a spiritual issue. America's foundations weren't built by chance, they were forged by the hands of the enslaved, laid one brick at a time beneath the whips of cruelty in the name of the law. Every monument, every institution, every inch of progress bears the shadow of their labor. And yet, the respect they were denied in life must not be denied in legacy.

The descendants of those enslaved are owed more than symbolic gestures. They are owed dignity, restitution, and the acknowledgment long withheld. Not just as a nod to history, but as an act of justice in the present. This is not charity, it's repair. It is accountability. It is the simple truth that greatness built on suffering can only be redeemed through reparation.

The nation cannot claim honor while ignoring its architects. The enslaved endured the unimaginable suffering to birth a country that proclaimed liberty while practicing bondage. Their descendants walk through the same halls they built, often still barred from the full promises they were encouraged to believe in.

Not only has there been no accountability for the atrocities of slavery, no restitution, no justice, and certainly no respect for the immeasurable contributions of Black American ancestors to this nation, but there has been a deliberate, systemic effort to keep their descendants bound. Whether through legislation, economic barriers, mass incarceration, or the distortion of history, the chains have been reforged in different forms, ensuring that freedom remains a constant battle rather than a guarantee.

This nation boldly declares itself the *Land of the Free*, yet bristles with indignation when the descendants of those who were enslaved, refuse to stand for its anthem. To demand reverence without reckoning is to build altars to ego, not truth. It's gaslighting with a straight face and an inward smirk.

The anthem that best reflects this nation's full story, its triumphs, yes, but also its wounds, is "Lift Every Voice and Sing." Written by James Weldon Johnson in 1900 and set to music by his brother J. Rosamond Johnson, its lyrics do not shy away from the "dark past," the "blood of the slaughtered," or the "chastening rod."

America should embrace the anthem that sings of its full journey, not just its victories, but its valleys. "Lift Every Voice and Sing" is not just a hymn. It is history. It is healing. It's sincere and truthful.

America must tear down its false altars, those monuments to myth, those anthems that sing of freedom while ignoring the chains. The national anthem, as it stands, is not a hymn of truth. It is a lullaby for the comfortable, a lie dressed in melody. It's an anthem that celebrates an evil past to make some people feel good.

The idol of white supremacy must be demolished, not debated. It is a false god that demands sacrifice: Truth and Justice. It has corrupted pulpits and courtrooms, textbooks, and legislation. And if America does not confront it, it will become consumed by it. This is not a political issue; it is a spiritual emergency. You cannot serve God and serve white supremacy. You cannot preach grace while defending oppression. The time for compromise is over. The altar must fall, or the nation will.

This is not a conservative or liberal issue. It transcends party lines, skin color, and socioeconomic status. This is a spiritual reckoning, a confrontation between humanity and God. Because injustice is not just a policy failure; it is a moral failure. And no amount of wealth, whiteness, or rhetoric can shield a nation from the consequences of unrepented sin. God is not moved by platforms; God is moved by righteousness. And until we stop debating symptoms and start confronting the soul, we will remain a nation out of alignment with heaven.

Chapter Seven – God Moves

Issue

How should Black Americans respond to persecution beneath the banner of justice? How should Black Americans respond when the law is used as a weapon while the crowd applauds our suffering? What do we do when our humanity is denied and our destruction is celebrated as order?

Introduction

A dark-skinned Middle Eastern Jewish man named Jesus, born into occupation, raised under oppression, and executed by the state, offers us some answers. Not with empire, but with empathy. Not with laws, but with love. Jesus stood with the marginalized, spoke truth to power, and declared justice as a holy calling.

History has long distorted the image of Jesus, portraying Him to the Black community as a blonde-haired, blue-eyed figure, a fabricated icon that bears little resemblance to reality. This deliberate misrepresentation has sustained the false narrative that Christianity is the religion of the "white man," leading many to turn away from the faith under the weight of cultural betrayal.

But the truth is clear: Jesus of Nazareth was never the product of Western ideals. His teachings defied empire, uplifted the oppressed, and confronted systems of control. Reclaiming His identity means reclaiming the liberating power of His message. Jesus is not a symbol of domination. He is a revolutionary figure whose truth transcends manipulation, whose love dismantles lies, and whose justice speaks directly to the wounded soul of Black America.

Jesus teaches Black Americans how to confront injustice when it wears the mask of legality.

In John 8:2–11, a woman is dragged before Jesus, publicly shamed, her life hanging in the balance, all under the guise of the law. Her accusers cite Scripture, weaponizing it to justify violence. But Jesus neither flinches nor condemns. Instead, Jesus exposes the hypocrisy of the legal system that claims righteousness while dealing in shame and death.

His response is a masterclass in divine resistance: "Let him who is without sin cast the first stone." With one sentence, Jesus disarms the mob, reframes justice, and restores dignity. For Black Americans, long victimized in the name of the law, this moment stands as a blueprint for confronting systems that use the law to justify oppression.

Jesus embodies the blueprint for justice. He spoke truth to power that dehumanized a woman, He shielded someone who was vulnerable, and He turned an unfair accusation into a pathway for liberation. The powerful people dropped their stones and walked away in shame.

Text

John 8:1-11 (Ethiopian Bible)

[1]Jesus went unto the mount of Olives. [2] And early in the morning he came again into the temple, and all the people came unto him; and he sat down, and taught them. [3] And the scribes and Pharisees brought unto him a woman taken in adultery; and when they had set her in the midst, [4] They say unto him, Master, this woman was taken in adultery, in the very act. [5] Now Moses in the law commanded us, that such should be stoned: but what sayest thou? [6] This they said, tempting him, that they might have to accuse him. But Jesus stooped down, and with his finger wrote on the ground, as though he heard them not. [7] So when they continued asking him, he lifted up himself, and said unto them, He that is without sin among you, let him first cast a stone at her. [8] And again he stooped down and wrote on the ground. [9] And they which heard it, being convicted by their own conscience, went out one by one, beginning at the eldest, even unto the last: and Jesus was left alone, and the woman standing in the midst. [10] When Jesus had lifted up himself, and saw none but the woman, he said unto her, Woman, where are those thine accusers? hath no man condemned thee? [11] She said, No man, Lord. And Jesus said unto her, Neither do I condemn thee: go, and sin no more. [12] Then spake Jesus again unto them, saying, I am the light of the world, he that followeth me shall not walk in darkness, but shall have the light of life.

Subject: In The Name of The Law

As Jesus taught in the Temple courtyard, the scribes and Pharisees, experts in the law, dragged a woman before Him, accusing her of adultery. She was not just on trial for her actions; she was a pawn in their plot to trap Jesus. They cited the law of Moses, demanding condemnation.

The law they were using against her is cited in Leviticus 20:10 (NIV): *"If a man commits adultery with another man's wife, with the wife of his neighbor, both the adulterer and the adulteress are to be put to death."*

According to the Levitical law, adultery was a sin that involved two parties, a man and a woman. Both were to be held accountable. But when the religious leaders brought forth the woman allegedly caught in adultery, the man was missing.

This omission was not an oversight. It exposed their hearts. Their accusation was not about justice; it was about entrapment. It was about manipulation. They twisted the law to serve their own agenda. The accusers were powerful men, making accusations against a woman.

The text is a powerful example of how laws can become tools of oppression rather than instruments of justice.

They were trying to trap Jesus, searching for any justification to arrest Him in front of His followers. Their plan hinged on forcing Him into a dilemma, either uphold the law and condemn the woman to death or show mercy and violate the law.

If Jesus showed compassion, they would pounce, accusing Him of defying divine law, eager to discredit His authority and hasten His downfall. But if He chose condemnation, they would gloat, satisfied that the one who preached mercy had become no different from them: enforcers of the law stripped of love.

They were weaponizing the law and exploiting a woman they deemed disposable. She was not a person to them, she was bait. Just a body, just a pawn. They were using her to serve their own agenda.

They were willing to watch her die, stoned to death, by their twisted interpretation of the law, and then blame Jesus.

Their arrogance was undeniable; they expected unquestioning acceptance of their allegations, even with insufficient evidence.

They assumed that their authority alone would be enough to condemn her. No trial. No evidence. Just accusation.

Their aim was not justice, it was destruction. They did not seek truth; they sought spectacle. In their hearts, mercy had no place. They wanted to drag her into the center and make her shame a public display. It was not the law they honored, but mob judgment. They wanted to lynch her.

The way they treated her sounds familiar, doesn't it?

In her story, we see the reflection of our modern criminal system. It targets Black Americans, using laws written for all but only applied to them.[33] The agenda is clear: to generate wealth through mass

---

[33] See Michelle Alexander, THE NEW JIM CROW: MASS INCARCERATION IN THE AGE OF COLORBLINDNESS 4–7 (2010); Laura I. Appleman, Bloody Lucre: Carceral Labor and Prison Profit, 2022 WIS. L. REV. 631–32 (detailing discriminatory application of Black Codes); Jason Taper, Legal Fellow at the Surveillance Technology Oversight Project (S.T.O.P.), In Response to Recent Report on NYPD Gang Database, G.A.N.G.S. Coalition Rallies to Abolish Harmful Policing Tool, Legal

incarceration, a modern extension of slavery rooted in the centuries of stolen labor that built this nation's foundation.[34]

For generations, the laws and media propaganda to support it, have been weaponized against Black Americans, designed not only to oppress but to shape perception. All of it has been used to paint Black communities as inferior, dangerous, and unworthy, distorting the way others see us, and even how we see ourselves.

This deliberate manipulation echoes the vision once set forth by Supreme Court Justice Taney, reinforcing the very barriers he sought to institutionalize. [35]Though time has marched on, his legacy of exclusion and control remains etched into the nation's legal foundation, sustained by systems that still resist justice and equity.[36]

This manipulation has been perfected and refined over the years, and

---

Defense Fund (Oct. 23, 2025) (noting database targets "98% Black and Latinx youth").

[34] See Laura I. Appleman, Bloody Lucre: Carceral Labor and Prison Profit, 2022 WIS. L. REV. 620–21, 630–32 (discussing how the South harnessed carceral labor for "maximum profits" and how profit is "inextricably intertwined" with the system); see also Alexander, supra note 1, at 4–5 (contending mass incarceration is a "well-disguised system of racialized social control").

[35] See Sandra L. Rierson, From Dred Scott to Anchor Babies: White Supremacy and the Contemporary Assault on Birthright Citizenship, 38 GEO. IMMIGR. L.J. 6, 6–16 (2023) (discussing how Chief Justice Taney's analysis in Dred Scott institutionalized a permanent caste of non-citizens).

[36] See Alexander, supra note 1, at 4–5 (describing mass incarceration as racialized social control); Laura I. Appleman, Bloody Lucre: Carceral Labor and Prison Profit, 2022 WIS. L. REV. 620–21 (explaining the continuous influence of the profit motive linked to slavery); Dred Scott v. Sandford, 60 U.S. (19 How.) 393 (1857) (providing foundational legal precedent for racial exclusion); cf. Rosewood massacre, Wikipedia (describing mass racial violence and subsequent failure to prosecute perpetrators in 1923).

the dehumanization of Black Americans makes it easier to dehumanize other groups of people in American and abroad.

It is the same spirit of injustice that once condemned a woman with no trial and no defense. But she did not remain in the dust. She walked away, not because the system granted mercy, but because of Jesus.

Jesus saw her.

Not their accusations.

Jesus did not look at her shame.

Jesus looked at her.

Jesus stood between power and the powerless, between law and love. In that moment, Jesus shattered the cycle of condemnation.

On that day, Jesus stood before power, not in fear, not in compromise, but in clarity and conviction. He did not allow the machinery of influence to define justice.

His response is instructive for us today.

Jesus sees us too.

Jesus has seen the spirit of injustice condemn Black Americans. He knows exactly what we have been through, and there will be an accounting for all that has happened.

But in the meantime, Jesus shows us how we should respond to injustice when it is wrapped in authority, and presented in the name of the law.

The first thing we learn is this:

(1) Stay Rooted in Truth, No Matter the Trap

John 8:5-7

[5] In the Law Moses commanded us to stone such women. Now what do you say?" [6] They were using this question as a trap, in order to have a basis for accusing him. But Jesus bent down and started to write on the ground with his finger. [7] [And] they kept on questioning him.

The Pharisees tried to manipulate Jesus into a no-win scenario, but He refused to play by their rules. He didn't react impulsively.

He responded with wisdom, exposing their hypocrisy.

This teaches us that when systems attempt to corner us, we must remain grounded in truth, using knowledge and strategy to dismantle injustice rather than falling into its snares.

Simply put: We must be better than they are. We cannot lower ourselves to their level.

Dehumanization has been our inheritance, and our resistance has taken many forms. At times, we have borne the weight in silence. At other times, the rage boiled over into rebellion. Neither path was easy, and neither should be judged without truth. Because when people are denied their humanity, the response is never simple, it is survival.

Chattel slavery was not just an institution; it was an assault on the soul. [37]Century after century, freedom sat just beyond the horizon, while Black lives were bought, broken, and buried under laws crafted to legitimize cruelty. [38]It was savage. It was demonic. And it refused to let freedom breathe.

It was not love that broke the chains. It was not conviction. It was strategy.

The enslaved were exploited as bargaining chips, tools to tilt power toward the North. Their liberation was not the goal; it was the

---

[37] See Laura I. Appleman, “Bloody Lucre: Carceral Labor and Prison Profit,” Wisconsin Law Review (2022): 620–21 (noting that the institution of slavery, alongside carceral labor, yielded "enormous proceeds through the transformation of human toil into financial gain" and was inextricably intertwined with the system of criminal punishment); see also Michelle Alexander, The New Jim Crow: Mass Incarceration in the Age of Colorblindness (New York: The New Press, 2010), 4–5 (explaining that modern mass incarceration is a "racialized social control that functions in a manner strikingly similar to Jim Crow", which creates a permanent "undercaste", reflecting the systemic and institutional denial of basic humanity inherent in chattel slavery).

[38] See Laura I. Appleman, “Bloody Lucre: Carceral Labor and Prison Profit,” Wisconsin Law Review (2022): 620–21, 630–32 (explaining that, along with the institution of slavery, involuntary carceral labor yielded "enormous proceeds through the transformation of human toil into financial gain"; detailing how laws like the Black Codes were used to subject Black citizens to carceral bondage, creating "an organized capital market for Black prisoners" who were often worked in brutal conditions, sometimes to death, with little incentive to preserve their lives); see also Michelle Alexander, The New Jim Crow: Mass Incarceration in the Age of Colorblindness (New York: The New Press, 2010), 4–5, 363 (contending that this resulting structure of exclusion is a "stunningly comprehensive and well-disguised system of racialized social control" that perpetuates an inferior position by law and custom).

consequence. [39]But even in that bitter transaction, God moved. The chains came loose, not because Black people were seen as human, but because an empire cracked.

The same God who broke the chains of chattel slavery can dismantle the bars of mass incarceration. What God did for our ancestors, God can do again, because God's power does not expire, and God's justice does not sleep.

Mass incarceration is the modern trap, a system designed to ensnare Black Americans under the guise of legality. [40]

---

[39] See Laura I. Appleman, "Bloody Lucre: Carceral Labor and Prison Profit," Wisconsin Law Review (2022): 620–21 (explaining that the institution of slavery, along with involuntary carceral labor, yielded "enormous proceeds through the transformation of human toil into financial gain"); see also Michelle Alexander, The New Jim Crow: Mass Incarceration in the Age of Colorblindness (New York: The New Press, 2010), 4–5; cf. Alexander, The New Jim Crow (discussing the persistently lingering result of the lack of land reform, where "the former slaves were not granted any of the property on which they had long labored... [and] ended up with nothing," demonstrating that liberation was incomplete and lacked economic empowerment).

[40] See Michelle Alexander, The New Jim Crow: Mass Incarceration in the Age of Colorblindness (New York: The New Press, 2010), 4–7 (describing mass incarceration as a "stunningly comprehensive and well-disguised system of racialized social control" that keeps people of color in an inferior position by law and custom and uses seemingly neutral policy to enforce discrimination); see also Laura I. Appleman, "Bloody Lucre: Carceral Labor and Prison Profit," Wisconsin Law Review (2022): 620–21, 630–32 (explaining that the system evolved from the "unaltering focus on money-making" and detailing how laws like the Black Codes were used to force Black citizens into "involuntary carceral labor" through racially discriminatory arrests and convictions, thus utilizing the guise of legality); cf. Jason Taper, Legal Fellow at the Surveillance Technology Oversight Project (S.T.O.P.), in "In Response to Recent Report on NYPD Gang Database, G.A.N.G.S. Coalition Rallies to Abolish Harmful Policing Tool," Legal Defense Fund, Oct. 23, 2025

But we have a model for how to respond when power lays a snare. When the religious and political elite tried to entrap Jesus, He did not flinch. He did not react impulsively or emotionally. He responded with divine restraint, bending down and writing on the ground, refusing to be rushed into their game. His silence spoke louder than their accusations. His timing shattered their trap.

Too often, we react too quickly and emotionally.

Emotions are real, but they are not always reliable. And when the stakes are high, and deception is near, God's people must learn the strength of a composed spirit. To think. To pray. To respond not with fire, but with focus.

When people set traps, our instinct may be to react, but wisdom calls us to pause and think. They tried to corner Jesus with pressure and urgency, yet Jesus refused to be rushed. He moved at His own pace, just like God does, intentional, unshaken, and guided by purpose.

This battle is not about personalities or politics, it's about spirit, influence, and truth. Listening to the Holy Spirit equips us with discernment when deception wears a friendly face. It teaches us when to speak, when to wait, and how to respond with power wrapped in grace.

The enemy thrives when we mistake spiritual warfare for personal

---

(providing a modern example where a system, using legal processes, surveils "98% Black and Latinx youth" and "can only be understood as a tool of racial discrimination").

grievance, when we try to fight fire with flesh instead of Spirit. But the Holy Spirit does not just whisper comfort, it declares strategy. It exposes traps. It illuminates the truth.

When powerful forces plot against us, our defense cannot be flesh, it must be Spirit. We need the power of the Holy Spirit to discern, to withstand, and to respond. That's why our prayers must be relentless, ongoing, unwavering, nonstop. As Paul declared in Ephesians 6:18: *"And pray in the Spirit on all occasions with all kinds of prayers and requests. With this in mind, be alert and always keep on praying for all the Lord's people."*

In a world of spiritual warfare, prayer is not optional, its armor. And the Spirit does not just comfort; It equips. This battle requires alertness, persistence, and divine strategy.

God has a move that is greater than any trap the enemy has set for us.

God still moves and God will move on our behalf.

The next thing we learn is that there will be a time for us to:

(2) Stand Up And Speak Up

John 8:7 NIV

[7] When they kept on questioning him, he straightened up and said to them, "Let any one of you who is without sin be the first to throw a stone at her."

Once the Holy Spirit reveals the plan, don't hesitate, stand up and speak up. But when you see a trap being set, do not let urgency override discernment.

Silence can be Spirit-led, just as speech can be Spirit-powered.

Wisdom knows when to wait and when to rise.

So Jesus did not get drawn into their trap.

They pressed Jesus for a legal verdict.

But Jesus did not address the professed reason they raised to trap Jesus: He did not say "Guilty" or "Not Guilty."

Jesus also did not address their hidden agenda: He did not take it personal and make it about him by saying something like, "I know you're trying to trap me."

He refused to validate their misuse of the law with an answer that fit their framework.

He changed the playing field.

They brought the law, the accusation, the woman, and demanded a verdict.

Jesus refused to play by their rules. Instead, he changed the rules entirely.

Instead, He dismantled the entire setup, not with accusation or defense, but with truth.

A truth so piercing it bypassed both their question and their motive: *"Let any one of you who is without sin be the first to throw a stone at her."*

He addressed the real issue. He unmasked hypocrisy and redirected the focus from punishment to reflection.

That was not just a clever reply. That was divine authority disrupting corrupted power.

And the same Spirit that guided Jesus in that moment still speaks today.

The Holy Spirit has every answer we need, not to react, but to respond with righteousness, clarity, and power.

In the same way, Black communities must continue to challenge laws and policies that are weaponized against them, exposing their flaws, demanding accountability, and reshaping legal systems to serve justice instead of oppression.

It is a power issue. *Our struggle is not against flesh and blood, but against the rulers, against the authorities, against the powers of this dark world and against the spiritual forces of evil in the heavenly realms.* (Ephesians 6:12)

Jesus stood up because silence was no longer strategic, truth had to be spoken. And when He did speak, He didn't argue law. With one sentence, He collapsed their hypocrisy, protected the vulnerable, and shifted the atmosphere.

When we wait on God and the Holy Spirit before we stand and speak, we arm ourselves with different weapons. Not with fists or fury, but with wisdom, truth, timing, and revelation. The Holy Spirit equips us with discernment that cuts deeper than accusation, and authority that outruns intimidation.

These are not earthly tools; they are divine strategies. It prevents us from responding because we've been provoked. We respond because we are led. And when the Spirit guides our words, the traps become testimonies.

The weapons we fight with are not the weapons of the world. On the contrary, our weapons have divine power to demolish strongholds. (2 Corinthians 10:4)

There is a stronghold in this country that worships the false god of white supremacy. This false god is worshipped by people of all colors, especially Black Americans.

And there is much fear surrounding this false god due to its historical violence. But we must always remember, '*The Lord is to be feared above all gods.* (1 Chronicles 16:25)

This is a spiritual war, and the battle *belongs to the Lord*!

Every idol, whether carved by culture, policy, or pride, *will bow down before God*!

But victory does not come through haste. It begins in the quiet, as we wait on the Holy Spirit, seeking not just courage, but divine instruction.

When the Spirit speaks and the moment comes, we must rise, not in recklessness, but in righteousness.

We *stand up* and *speak up* armed with wisdom that confounds traps, truth that breaks strongholds, and authority that doesn't flinch.

Because when the move is Spirit-led, the result is never just noise, it's *liberation*!

Finally, the third thing we learn is that we must:

(3) Refuse To Let Others Define Your Worth

After the powerful men walked away, Jesus turned to the woman and spoke to her.

John 8:10-11

Jesus said, "Woman, where are they? Has no one condemned you?"
"No one, sir," she said.
Jesus responded:
"Then neither do I condemn you,"
"Go now and leave your life of sin."

This whole ordeal began because the Pharisees wanted to strip Jesus of His authority by discrediting Him publicly, but Jesus refused to let their attempts shake His mission.

The powerful, cloaked in authority and self-righteousness, had set a trap designed to strike down two targets with one cruel blow: the ministry of Jesus, and a woman they viewed as disposable, a mere instrument in their scheme, stripped of dignity and worth.

The woman was objectified as bait, just as the *Dred Scott* decision codified the refusal to recognize Black humanity.[41] The comparison underscores that this is not just a story of ancient cruelty, it mirrors systemic patterns that persist when law is weaponized against the vulnerable.

In that dusty courtyard, Jesus does more than shield a woman, he indicts a system. He bent low, not to ignore her accusers, but to expose their hypocrisy. His silence at that time, spoke louder than their laws. In refusing to play their game, Jesus did not just save her life; he reclaimed her humanity.

Just as the *Dred Scott* decision denied the image of God in Black bodies, this moment lays bare the danger of law divorced from mercy, power detached from compassion.[42]

God's message to Black Americans is to stand firm in their God-given value and their God-given purpose. Refuse to let false narratives dictate their worth or potential. Power will always try to control the oppressed, but resistance, truth, and dignity are what dismantle its grip.

The *rulers of this dark world* painted white faces black and acted sub-

---

[41] See Dred Scott v. Sandford, 60 U.S. (19 How.) 393 (1857); Alexander, supra note 1, at 4–5 (positing that mass incarceration functions as a "stunningly comprehensive and well-disguised system of racialized social control").

[42] See Dred Scott v. Sandford, 60 U.S. (19 How.) 393 (1857); Appleman, supra note 2, at 620–21 (explaining how profit warps the criminal justice system); Alexander, supra note 1, at 4–5 (describing mass incarceration as a system of racialized social control where "power detached from compassion" is normalized).

human to send false messages into the Universe in its attempt to destroy the image of God that resides in Black Americans.

The *authorities of this dark world* hijacked the music and entertainment industry to promote idolatry that targeted Black Americans to draw as many of them away from God as possible.

The *powers of this dark world* infiltrated newspapers, magazines, social media and other media outlets to bombard the atmosphere with negative stereotypes to cement the image that Black Americans are sub-human.

The *spiritual forces of evil in the heavenly realm* indoctrinated every child in the public school system to believe that Black Americans deserved to be slaves and treated like animals.

Black Americans face relentless attacks from every direction, aimed at defaming their character and redefining their identity.

Stone throwers have destroyed communities across the country in such places as Memphis, Tennessee, Atlanta, Georgia, Tulsa, Oklahoma, Corbin, Kentucky, Rosewood, Florida, and many more. [43]These communities were not just destabilized, they were incinerated. Homes burned, lives lost, and futures stolen in

[43] See, e.g., Rosewood massacre, Wikipedia (describing the 1923 event as a "racially motivated massacre of Black people"); cf. Alexander, supra note 1, at 4–5 (contending that mass incarceration is a system of racialized social control that followed the earlier Jim Crow era violence).

orchestrated acts of terror masquerading as law and order.[44]

Stone throwers come in every shade, melanated and non-melanated, because the spirit that seduces hearts toward evil has no respect for skin color. It is the condition of the soul that matters.

White supremacy, the idol enthroned in this nation, tempts most fiercely those who are groomed to benefit from its power. [45]Yet many Black Americans bow to it too. Some offer their worship through violence against their own, others through quiet disavowal and abandonment.

In a culture where false idols command loyalty, where white supremacy seduces hearts across color lines, the woman in John 8 stands as both symbol and mirror. She was dragged into the center by those who had pledged allegiance to legalism and control. Yet in that moment, Jesus did not reflect the corruption around Him; He revealed a different kingdom. He saw her. He paused. And in doing so, He exposed the cowardice of the crowd and reclaimed her humanity.

This divine refusal to play by oppressive rules is the very posture

---

[44] See Rosewood massacre, Wikipedia (detailing how a white mob "burned almost every structure in Rosewood," and the subsequent all-White grand jury "found insufficient evidence to prosecute any perpetrators," demonstrating legal failure); cf. Alexander, supra note 1, at 4–5 (positing that racialized social control includes violence and legal inaction).

[45] See Laura I. Appleman, Bloody Lucre: Carceral Labor and Prison Profit, 2022 WIS. L. REV. 620–21, 630–32 (explaining the criminal justice system was created to harness Black carceral labor for "maximum profits, feeding the material interests of prosperous white citizens"); see also Alexander, supra note 1, at 4 (contending that mass incarceration sustains a "racial caste system," maintained by those privileged by the structure).

Black Americans must reclaim, a resistance rooted not in ego or retaliation, but in the radical act of seeing and standing.

No stones were thrown against this woman because Jesus saw her worth. He was not moved by fear or ego. He saw her humanity and refused to let the stone throwers define it.

The stone bearers had already sentenced her without trial, despite the glaring absence of the man who, by law, should have stood beside her.

Their pursuit was not justice; it was spectacle. She was never meant to be heard, only used.

Even if she had shared that bed with a married man, her sin did not define her story. It was the system, the accusers, the silent crowd, the absent man, that tried to brand her by a moment.

Jesus refused to reduce her to a transaction. And so must we. We are not the sum of our failings. We must refuse to let our sins, or anyone else's condemnation of them, define who we are. God defined us before any accusation, before any failure, before any law was written. We were formed in His image, endowed with dignity that no courtroom, no policy, no history can erase.

The woman in John 8 was seen through that lens by Jesus, not as damaged goods, but as divine design. And that is the standard we must reclaim.

There is no power in judging others, or in letting their judgment define who we are. Instead, we must learn from Jesus. He saw sin but did not weaponize it. He saw brokenness and responded with truth and grace. We must recognize our own sins and understand that we stand in no position to condemn anyone else. But repentance is possible. Change is possible.

We were never meant to live shackled to shame. The way forward is not through judgment, it is through reckoning, redemption, and renewal.

We are in a spiritual war, make no mistake about it. The enemy is not flesh and blood, but principalities, powers, and systems designed to crush truth. Our weapons must be spiritual: prayer that pierces through darkness, truth that unmasks lies, and love that resists hatred. This battle belongs to the Lord, and the war is already won. But victory does not mean we stand idle. It means we armor up. It means we show up. It means we prepare our hearts and sharpen our voices. Because every day, the battlefield is real, and we must be ready when God moves.

CHRIST

The war was won on the old rugged cross. When Jesus surrendered His life, it looked like defeat to the powerful, Friday afternoon felt like victory to the empire, and they celebrated through the night. But on Sunday morning, death lost its grip. Jesus rose, and in His rising, He declared once and for all: injustice will not have the final word. The cross crushed the systems that seek to destroy, and the resurrection revealed the true power of redemption.

Jesus spoke first to Mary Magdalene, a woman deemed powerless by the world, yet powerful in the kingdom. Her value was not measured by status, but by her usefulness to God. She was chosen not because she was prominent, but because she was faithful.

To the powerful of this world, Black Americans may appear powerless, targeted, criminalized, and condemned in the name of the law. But in the eyes of God, we are vessels of divine purpose. Our power is not in social positioning, it is in spiritual usefulness. And in this war, this sacred, unseen war, we do not fight alone. The battle belongs to the Lord. And because Jesus rose, we rise too.

Epilogue

Fighting systemic injustice through spiritual warfare means engaging both the "seen and unseen realms," recognizing that oppressive systems are not just political or economic, but also deeply spiritual. Here are some powerful strategies rooted in faith, scripture, and community action:

🛡 1. Prayer as Protest

- Intercessory prayer targets spiritual strongholds behind injustice (2 Corinthians 10:3-6, Ephesians 6:12).

- Pray for discernment, boldness, and hearts to change, especially among leaders and institutions.

- Use lament as a spiritual tool to grieve injustice and call on God's justice (Exodus 2:23, Psalm 10, Psalm 94).

🔥 2. Prophetic Action

- Speak truth to power with prophetic courage, like the biblical prophets who condemned exploitation and injustice (Isaiah 1:17, Amos 5:7-24).

- Combine spiritual conviction with activism (march, vote, write, and organize) for reform, with a heart grounded in God's justice. (Psalm 11:7, Galatians 6:9)

□ 3. Spiritual Mapping & Repentance

- Identify spiritual roots of injustice in your community, historic oppression, economic exploitation, racial violence. (Judges 19, Luke 4:18-19)

- Practice repentance: confessing sins of the community and standing in the gap (Daniel 9, Nehemiah 1).

- Break generational curses and territorial spirits through strategic prayer and fasting. (Deuteronomy 28, Matthew 17:14-21)

🕊 4. Armor of God & Inner Transformation

- Equip yourself with the Full armor of God (Ephesians 6:10–18): truth, righteousness, peace, faith, salvation, and the Word.

- Resist bitterness and hatred - spiritual warfare is not against people, but against the forces that dehumanize and divide. (Acts 8:9-25, Ephesians 4:31)

- Cultivate joy, humility, and forgiveness as weapons against despair and division. (Philippians 4:8, 1 John 8-9)

□ 5. Build Spirit-Filled Communities

- Create spaces of healing, accountability, and resistance churches, small groups, justice ministries. (Luke 8:1-3, Acts 5:1-11)

- Engage in discipleship that confronts racism, teaches reconciliation, and empowers the oppressed. (John 4:1-26, Acts 11:1-18)

- Support restorative justice efforts that prioritize healing over punishment. (John 8:1-11, Acts 9:1-19)

📖 6. Scripture as Strategy

- Use the Bible to reframe justice: God's justice is restorative, not retributive. Hebrews 11

- Meditate on passages like Micah 6:8, Luke 4:18–19, and James 2:1–

9.

- Let scripture shape your worldview, not just your personal morality. (Matthew 5:14, Romans 12:2)

□ 7. Expose and Disarm Idolatry

- Racism and profit-driven justice systems are often rooted in idolatry — worship of power, money, and control. (Galatians 5:19-23, 1 Timothy 6:10)

- Spiritual warfare involves tearing down these idols (2 Corinthians 10:4–5, 1 John 5:21).

- Challenge narratives that dehumanize others and elevate self-interest.

Closing Prayer

Eternal God,

We come before You, humbled by the truths revealed in these pages.

You are the Judge who sees beyond courts, beyond legislation, into every hidden place.

Let the chains forged by greed and injustice be broken, not only in steel cells, but in spiritual strongholds.

Let the cries of the forgotten reach heaven and stir change on Earth.

Expose every lie masked as law, and the loophole twisted by profit,

Replace the love of money with the pursuit of mercy, justice, and truth.

May this work plant seeds of holy rebellion against evil,

Empower every reader to discern and resist spiritual wickedness in high places,

And remind us that in Your kingdom, no soul is disposable and no truth too dangerous.

God in Heaven, seal this message with divine conviction,

And let it be a call to warfare, not with fists, but with faith.

We close this book with hearts heavy and eyes open.

Its pages have laid bare a system bound by greed, one that hungers for bodies as currency and uses the law as a cloak for cruelty.

But we remember Your Son, Jesus, arrested without cause, falsely accused, tried by corrupt powers, and sentenced to die though innocent.

He was mocked, beaten, and crucified by a world addicted to authority and blind to justice. Yet in that suffering, He carried more than the weight of injustice. He bore the sins of the world.

And through that cross, He showed us the way:

That true power lies in sacrifice, not oppression;

That redemption is born of mercy, not money.

So now, let this book be a spark of holy discontent.

Let its message stir minds, awaken consciences, and call warriors of light to the frontlines.

May the example of Jesus inspire the courage to speak truth in systems that silence. May His resurrection remind us that even the most brutal machinery of injustice cannot bury righteousness forever.

We declare war on spiritual wickedness, not by might, but by Your Spirit. Let Your justice roll down like waters, and we will never forget that Jesus was a victim of a system that did not care about truth and justice, but your love raised Him from the dead, and the power of the resurrection is able to transform the ungodly system this world worships.

So, I pray this, not in the name of the law, but in the name that is above all names, Jesus! The name that still breaks chains!

Amen!

Dr. Gloria's Upcoming Books

COMING SOON!

How to Break Chains & Walk in Freedom: Spiritual Warfare Strategies Spiritual warfare strategies that will bring you out bondage, whether its addictive behavior or something else. There is a blueprint for success that comes straight from the Old and New Testaments in the Bible.

Women Useful to God in Powerful Ways A series of motivational sermons that demonstrate how useful anyone can be to God no matter who you are or where you have been or what you have done. The sermons are based on the lives of women who were military leaders, wives, prostitutes and more. Anyone can be useful to God.

We Can All Win! Everyone acts like this world has limited resources and the only way that they can get ahead in life is walk over someone else, cheat or to play dirty to win. You don't have to do any of those things, just trust God. If we all trusted God, this world would be a much better place. It can start with you.

Made in the USA
Monee, IL
12 November 2026

f83b6b59-c12d-4be0-840d-2ac95a112a43R01